ELEMENTARY

Reading Level: 1-3
Interest Level: 4–6

SCIENCE AND TECHNOLOGY

The Great Outdoors

COMPLETE SET OF 4 BOOKS: $105.08 / **$78.80** • 978-1-9785-3206-9
INDIVIDUAL TITLES: $26.27 / **$19.70**

8 ½" x 11" • 32 pp. • Full-Color Photographs and Illustrations

There are many ways to explore the great outdoors and many sights to see, and readers take journeys to the garden, the seashore, the forest, and the watery worlds of lakes and ponds in these fun and fact-filled guides. Informative and engaging main text is presented in a captivating style with colorful images of each outdoor landscape. Fun fact boxes ask readers to examine what they know and what they can learn about the world outside, and an age-appropriate quiz at the end of each volume allows them to develop their reading comprehension skills.

- *Sidebars feature fun activities themed to each outdoor location, including crafts and recipes explained with step-by-step instructions*
- *The creative and captivating design combines full-color photographs and beautiful illustrations*
- *Readers are encouraged to develop and explore their curiosity about the natural world, and they're also shown different ways to protect the environment and each ecosystem they learn about*

1. **Forest** EN1247
Lisa Regan • Library-Bound: 978-1-9785-3084-3
eBook: 978-1-9785-3085-0 • GRL: T • DEWEY: • ATOS: PENDING • ©2023

2. **Garden** EN1248
Lisa Regan • Library-Bound: 978-1-9785-3088-1
eBook: 978-1-9785-3089-8 • GRL: T • DEWEY: • ATOS: PENDING • ©2023

3. **Lakes and Ponds** EN1249
Lisa Regan • Library-Bound: 978-1-9785-3092-8
eBook: 978-1-9785-3093-5 • GRL: T • DEWEY: • ATOS: PENDING • ©2023

4. **Seashore** EN1250
Lisa Regan • Library-Bound: 978-1-9785-3096-6
eBook: 978-1-9785-3097-3 • GRL: T • DEWEY: • ATOS: PENDING • ©2023

NEW for Fall 2022!

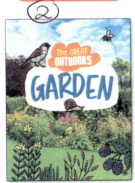
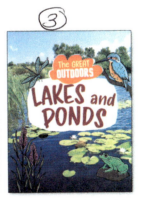
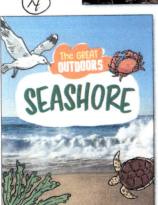

Actual Type Size

The GREAT OUTDOORS

FOREST

LISA REGAN

Published in 2023 by Enslow Publishing, LLC
29 East 21st Street, New York, NY 10010

Copyright © 2019 Wayland, a division of Hachette Children's Group

Editor: John Hort
Design and Illustrations: Supriya Sahai

All rights reserved. No part of this book may be reproduced
in any form without permission in writing from the publisher, except by a reviewer.

Please visit our website, www.enslowpublishing.com. For a free color catalog of all our high-quality books,
call toll free 1-800-398-2504 or fax 1-877-980-4454.

Cataloging-in-Publication Data

Title: Forest / Lisa Regan.
Description: New York : Enslow Publishing, 2023. | Series: The great outdoors | Includes glossary and index.
Identifiers: ISBN 9781978530829 (pbk.) | ISBN 9781978530843 (library bound) | ISBN 9781978530836 (6pack) | ISBN 9781978530850 (ebook)
Subjects: LCSH: Forest ecology--Juvenile literature. | Forests and forestry--Juvenile literature.
Classification: LCC QH541.5.F6 R438 2023 | DDC 577.3--dc23

Picture credits:

All images Shutterstock: Smileus 4a; Maxim Krivonos 6a; Pixel-Shot 6b; By Merkushev Vasiliy 6c; Steve Cordory 8a; Vi Mak 9a; sirtravelalot 10a; Lukiyanova Natalia frenta 10b; Coatesy 11a; HHC Images 11b; serkan mutan 12a; belu gheorghe 12b; Anna Hoychuk 13a; bjul 14a; Tunatura 15a; Eric Isselee 16a; Rudmer Zwerver 16b; LazyFocus 16c; Drakuliren 17a; Vlada Cech 17b; Stephan Morris 17c; Steve Byland 17d; Anan Kaewkhammul 17e; Ronnie Howard 17f; Tim Zurowski 18a; Tony Campbell 18b; Mark Bridger 18c; picturepartners 18d; magnetix 18e; Marcin Perkowski 19a;YK 19b; EvgenyPopov 19c; Coatesy 19d; Serjio74 19e; Svetlana Zhukova 20a; PhotoHouse 20b; Tatyana Mi 20c; Olga_V 20d; Johannes Kornelius 20e; anyaivanova 20f; mirkciuke1042 21a; Peter Turner Photography 21b; Bonnie Watton 21c; Richard Griffin 21d; Mark Herreid 21e; Kichigin 22a; Vlad Sokolovsky 23a; TalyaPhoto 24a; Sandra Standbridge 25a; Perutskyi Petro 25b; Frank Cornelissen 26a; Quietword 27a; Lucky-photographer 28a; Rich Carey 29a

Manufactured in the United States of America

CPSIA compliance information: Batch #CSENS23: For further information contact
Enslow Publishing LLC, New York, New York at 1-800-398-2504.

Find us on

CONTENTS

What is a woodland?	4
From seed to tree	6
Life-giving leaves	8
Through the seasons	10
Deciduous forests	12
Evergreen forests	14
Woodland creatures	16
Woodland birds	18
Woodland flowers	20
Woodland wonders	22
What's in a log?	24
Finding food	26
Protecting our woodlands	28
Quiz	30
Glossary	31
Index and further reading	32

WHAT IS A WOODLAND?

Trees are everywhere. A woodland is a collection of hundreds, thousands, or even millions of trees together. Woods and forests are both areas of woodland, and forests are usually bigger than woods. Woodlands provide a home to all sorts of plants and creatures.

How green are your trees?
Look at the trees at different times of year. Do you notice any big differences? There are two types of tree: **deciduous** and **evergreen.** In autumn, the leaves of deciduous trees change from green to red, orange, and brown. Then they lose their leaves altogether. Evergreen trees keep their leaves all year round. Many evergreen trees are **conifers**, which bear cones and have thin, pointed needles as leaves.

From small beginnings
It takes many years for a woodland to grow. Small plants appear first and are gradually overtaken by bigger plants, causing changes in the soil. Eventually the biggest trees fill the space.

DID YOU KNOW?
The stages of growth are called "succession."

Year 1: Bare ground and weeds
This is how it begins. Hardy flowers such as dandelions and ragweed take root.

Year 2: Grasses and plants
Grasses start to grow, followed by ferns and bracken.

Years 3–5: Shrubland
Thicker-stemmed bushes and shrubs take over from the grasses.

Around the world

There are three major forest zones, separated according to their distance from the equator. Tropical rainforests grow in hot, wet places near the equator. Temperate forests cover large parts of North America, Europe, and northern Asia, where there are four separate seasons. Colder parts of these continents have boreal forests, also called taiga, made up mostly of evergreen trees.

- tropical rainforest
- temperate forest
- boreal forest

Years 6–15: Saplings
Young, skinny trees fight for space to grow.

Years 16–50: Young woodland
Small trees begin to rise above the other plants. They get more sunlight and cast shade below.

Year 51 onward: Mature woodland
The biggest trees are now thick and strong. Sometimes a large tree dies so more sunlight reaches the layers underneath.

FROM SEED TO TREE

Even the biggest trees begin as a small seed. You may have seen some already: acorns, chestnuts, and sycamore wings are all seeds. Coniferous trees keep their seeds tucked inside cones—they are often called pine cones.

Starting small

When the seed falls onto suitable soil and germinates, it puts out a root and a shoot. Using food energy stored in the acorn, the shoot pushes up through the soil and out into the sunlight. Special leaves open out. Now it is a sapling.

The mighty oak

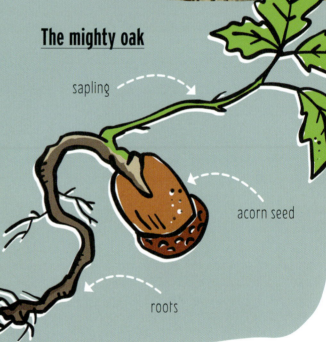

sapling

acorn seed

roots

sycamore wings

Getting around

If a seed falls close to its mother tree, it may not have room to grow. It is better for the seeds to be spread far and wide. Many seeds fly on the wind or float on the water. Others, in the form of nuts and fruits, are tasty treats for animals. Many animals take seeds to a completely different location to store them..

horse chestnut

On the outside

The tough outer layer of a trunk is called bark. It keeps the tree safe from animals and holds moisture inside. It also protects the tree from the elements and from fungus and diseases. It is actually a layer of dead wood. It cannot stretch as the tree grows, which is what gives it its cracks, lines, and patterns.

TRY THIS...

GROW YOUR OWN OAK TREE

Gather acorns when they fall to the ground and watch them sprout.

- Choose one that is plump, not dried up, and put it in a sandwich bag with some damp leaves and dirt.
- Store it (unsealed) in the fridge until spring, and then plant it.
- Punch holes in the bottom of a foam cup and fill it with potting compost. Place the acorn on its side.
- Keep it well watered in a sunny spot. It should begin to sprout after about three weeks.

In the rings

Look carefully at the stump of a fallen or chopped-down tree. You will see various sections that show how the tree has grown bigger and stronger over the years.

The oldest part of the tree is called the **heartwood** and is dead.

The paler, living rings are younger and are called **sapwood**.

Tiny tubes inside the bark carry food from the leaves to the rest of the tree.

Marks in the rings show damage from disease, injuries, pollution, and forest fires.

Just inside the bark is the **cambium** that makes the trunk grow stronger each year.

The bark can be very thin or very thick, depending on the type of tree.

DID YOU KNOW?
Each year of growth is seen as a new ring of wood.

LIFE-GIVING LEAVES

Trees and other plants use their leaves to make their own food. The leaves make sugar using energy from sunlight, carbon dioxide gas, and water. This process is called **photosynthesis**, and it makes the food a plant needs to grow.

A simple broad leaf

apex or tip

margin

blade

veins

midrib

Leaf lesson

There are two main types of leaf. Deciduous trees usually have broad leaves, while evergreens usually have narrow leaves called needles. Broad leaves can be lots of different shapes. Some are **compound leaves**, made up of several smaller leaflets, but many are **simple leaves** with a single piece.

A compound broad leaf

petiole

Take a look

A broad leaf has veins on it. These carry food through the leaf to other parts of the tree. They also act like a skeleton, making the leaf stronger. In summer, broad leaves are mostly green because of a substance inside called chlorophyll. This is a chemical that helps it absorb light, which is used to make food by photosynthesis.

All shapes and sizes

Different shapes of leaf are suited to different conditions, such as hot or cold and wet or dry. They also have different-shaped edges, or margins: Some are smooth, others are toothed, and some are wobbly or lobed, like an oak leaf.

A conifer's needles also make food. They don't fall off every year; instead, they stay on the tree for up to five years.

OVAL
(apple, beech)

LOBED
(oak, maple)

HEART-SHAPED
(hazel, common lime)

JAGGED
(hawthorn, sycamore)

TRIANGULAR
(birch, cottonwood)

NARROW
(willow, sweet chestnut)

TRY THIS...

MAKE A LEAF RUBBING

Capture the gorgeous patterns of nature for your home.

- Collect fallen leaves in as many different shapes as you can find.
- Lay them face down on a piece of paper (so the veins are facing upward). Place another piece of white paper on top.
- Use the long side of a crayon to gently rub over the leaves.

THROUGH THE SEASONS

If you watch a woodland through a whole year, you will see all sorts of changes take place. There will be lots of other seasonal activity that you can't easily see, with animals going about their business as the months go by.

Bees and butterflies collect nectar in summer.

Summer

The wood or forest floor is in shade as the trees are full of leaves. You can hear birds everywhere. Some of them will have flown here for the summer (this is called **migration**).

Spring

Things burst into life in spring. Many baby animals are born. Birds gather twigs to build their nests, ready to lay eggs. The woodland floor is covered with flowers, and buds appear on the bare trees.

Predators such as weasels may try to steal eggs from a nest.

A hedgehog hibernates

Time to sleep

Some woodland creatures eat through the harvest to get as fat as they can, and then slow down to save energy. Others actually sleep for weeks until winter has passed. Their heart beats more slowly and their body temperature drops. It is known as **hibernation**, and chipmunks, bats, hedgehogs, snakes, and some turtles and frogs do it. Other animals, such as bears, raccoons, and skunks sleep lightly, waking every so often to grab a snack.

Autumn

Leaves lose their chlorophyll, turning from green to shades of gold, brown, and red. Plants produce nuts and berries to spread their seeds. This gives animals the chance to feast and store food for the winter.

Winter buds will become new shoots in the spring.

Winter

Deciduous trees lose their leaves, but winter snowdrops and evergreen plants such as holly, hawthorn, and ferns stop the woodland from becoming completely bare. Animals snuggle into their dens and nests to stay warm.

DECIDUOUS FORESTS

Deciduous trees grow best in areas that are wet and mild (not too hot or too cold). They are found in a broad band across the northern hemisphere, in North America, Europe, and eastern Asia. Plants and creatures that live there have to adapt to the changing seasons.

Losing leaves

Most of the trees in deciduous forests lose their leaves in autumn. It helps them keep precious stores of water and energy. The tallest deciduous trees are oak, ash, birch, maple, elm, beech, linden, walnut, and larch. Larches are unusual: They are conifers, but they lose their needles each year.

Birds of prey, like this kestrel, nest high in the treetops.

Younger trees try to get enough sunlight to grow beneath the higher canopy of leaves and branches.

Many shrubs also grow, such as mountain laurel, huckleberries, and rhododendrons.

rhododendron

DID YOU KNOW?

The lack of leaves on trees makes it easier for pollen to spread in the springtime.

TRY THIS...

MAKE A BUG HOME

Lots of beetles, lacewings, and other creepy crawlies sleep through the winter.

You can make a warm, safe hiding place for them. Find a quiet, sheltered spot and make a pile of fallen sticks, leaves, and pine cones. It might not look like much to you, but it will be a safe haven for bugs in bad weather.

Home Sweet Home

Tree squirrels make their home in the trunks, and ground squirrels run around far below.

Many insects lay their eggs before winter. The eggs hatch when spring brings warmer temperatures.

The floor is a home to ferns, mosses, lichens, fungi, and lots of creatures, from frogs and snakes to spiders and centipedes.

EVERGREEN FORESTS

Evergreen forests are made up mostly of conifers—trees with cones and needles. They survive long, snowy winters and warm summers, and they are often located near mountain ranges or the coast. You can find these forests in North America, Europe, and Asia.

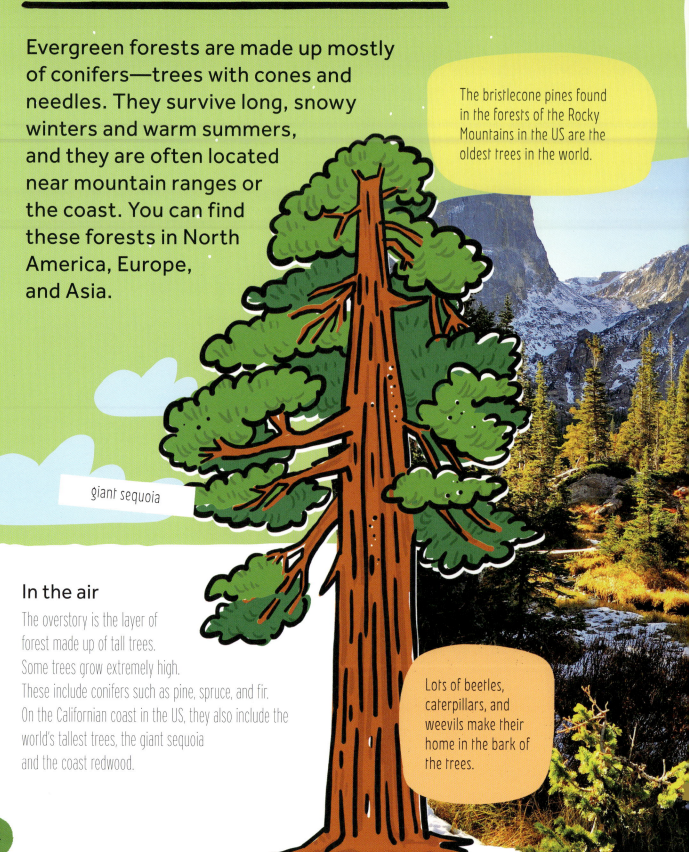

giant sequoia

The bristlecone pines found in the forests of the Rocky Mountains in the US are the oldest trees in the world.

Lots of beetles, caterpillars, and weevils make their home in the bark of the trees.

In the air

The overstory is the layer of forest made up of tall trees. Some trees grow extremely high. These include conifers such as pine, spruce, and fir. On the Californian coast in the US, they also include the world's tallest trees, the giant sequoia and the coast redwood.

Swarms of gnats can be a problem in these forests.

The forests provide shelter for large wild animals, from bears, mountain lions, and wolves to deer, moose, and beavers.

The floor may be covered by mosses or fungi, which grow well in the shade.

TRY THIS...

PREDICT THE WEATHER

Take a closer look at pine cones to see if it's going to rain.

- Collect a handful of fallen cones. Gather different shapes and sizes.
- Tie cotton thread around the pine cones and hang them outside your window. Check them every day.

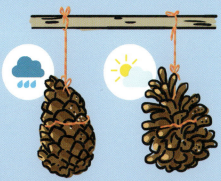

- A pine cone's outer scales swell in damp conditions and close up, to keep in their seeds. Tightly-shut scales mean rain, and open scales are a sign of dry weather to come.

On the ground

The understory is made up of smaller shrubs and grasses, plus a carpet of dry twigs, needles, and some leaf litter. There is a high danger of forest fires, which destroy large areas. It is not always disastrous; some plants, such as the lodgepole pine, need fire for their seeds to be released, and the ashes from burned trees add nutrients to the soil. For this reason, experts will sometimes do controlled burns to set only certain areas on fire.

WOODLAND CREATURES

All sorts of creatures are found in woodlands. Lots of woodland animals are shy and difficult to find, but they often leave behind signs that they were there, such as fur, footprints, feces, or damage to tree trunks.

Deer
You might spot these shy creatures through the forest trees. There are many different types of deer, and they are all most active early in the morning or late in the evening. They eat all sorts of plants, from apples and flowers to bark and grass.

Wolf
Endangered red wolves live in the deciduous forests of the USA. Grey wolves roam widely through many northern forests and hunt in packs for animals such as moose, elk, and deer.

gray wolf

Brown bear
These giants live in the coniferous and deciduous forests of North America, Europe, and Asia. They look fierce but eat a large quantity of nuts, fruit, berries, and roots. They dig a den to hibernate and have their cubs before spring.

Coyote
Only found in North America, these animals are related to wolves. They hunt small mammals but also eat fruit and grass.

Porcupine
You may be surprised to learn that these prickly North American animals can climb trees! They eat leaves, twigs, bark and small green plants.

Weasel
This slender creature is the smallest **carnivore** (meat eater) in the world. Its coat changes from brown to white in the winter.

Beaver
Beavers live in the water but have to be near trees to make their dams and lodges. You might just spot one swimming, or you could always look out for their building work.

Fox
The red fox is a dawn and dusk hunter, but easier to spot as they will happily leave the forest and look for food near houses and streets.

TRY THIS...

ANIMAL TRACKING
Learn to read the signs left behind by our wild friends.

- Walk slowly along a woodland path, looking to each side of you. Pay particular attention to flattened grass or muddy patches.

- Can you see footprints? What direction are they leading in? Can you identify what animal made them?

- Keep a record in a notebook. Draw the prints or glue in a photo. Add the date, time, and weather conditions.

- Look for other animal clues, such as nibbled nuts, fur caught on a fence, or pellets of poo.

- Always wash your hands properly after a nature walk.

Moose
Found in deciduous forests in the northern US, Canada, and Russia, moose (also called elk) have huge, hand-shaped antlers. They eat leaves, twigs, buds and cones, and bark. Look for trunks that have strips of bark peeled off.

WOODLAND BIRDS

As you walk through the trees, there will be hundreds of birds perching, nesting, and feeding all around you. Choose a sheltered position, sit quietly, and you will be rewarded with lots of birdsong. You will also probably spot many birds.

barn owl

Owl
There are lots of different types of owl, and many of them live in the woods. They make their nest in tree hollows and hunt for small creatures.

Finch
A finch is a small bird with a forked tail and quite a chubby round body. Its beak is short and triangular to make eating seeds easier. There are many types in a variety of lovely colors.

female and male American goldfinches

This pellet is the undigested parts of an owl's food, coughed up through its beak.

female and male turkeys

Crossbill
This bird is a member of the finch family that has a specially shaped beak for feeding on the cones of conifer trees.

red crossbill

Turkey
The turkey is a member of the pheasant family that is found in the forests of North America. They sleep in trees to stay safe from predators.

Grouse
Most types of grouse are medium-sized birds with a neat head and plump body. They can often be seen on the ground, pecking at plants and seeds.

Capercaillie
This bird is becoming rare, but is a very distinctive sight around conifer forests in northern Europe and Asia. It is the largest in the grouse family.

Bald eagle
Found in the forests of Canada and parts of the US, the bald eagle roosts and nests in both types of forest. It must live near water, though, to feed on fish.

great spotted woodpecker

Woodpecker
Listen carefully for the drumming sound a woodpecker makes against the trunk of a tree in the spring. At other times, you might hear its call, which sounds like "kek-kek" or "pik-pik" over and over.

Pheasant
These birds nest on the ground and prefer to run rather than fly. Usually seen in open fields, they roost in woodland trees and bushes. Pheasants originated from Asia and are found in forests worldwide now.

TRY THIS...

BIRD WATCHING

If you keep still and quiet for some time, you should see a variety of birds in woodlands.

- Take a sketchbook with you. It is often better to draw a bird than to try to photograph it among the trees. Draw the bird from different angles.

- Note down as much detail as you can: size, beak shape, different markings, how the bird moves, and what sounds it makes.

- Never disturb or remove eggs or nests. You should not pick up feathers either, even if you find them on the ground. This is illegal according to the Migratory Bird Treaty Act.

 Many bird footprints have three toes at the front and one behind.

WOODLAND FLOWERS

A woodland walk can reveal many beautiful flowers as you wander, depending on the kind of woods or forest you visit. Evergreen forests have fewer flowers than deciduous forests, as the conditions there are generally harsher.

Lily of the valley
The bell-shaped flowers of this plant are white, and it has a strong perfumed smell. Be careful, though, as it is poisonous.

Goldenrod
This plant has bright yellow flowers in the summer and attracts lots of bees, butterflies, and other insects.

Wild rose
Wild roses like the Nootka rose and the dog rose grow at the edge of forests. Their berries are called hips, and they grow in winter. The bushes have pretty pink flowers with five petals.

Wood sorrel
Look for the leaves of this plant to identify it. It has three heart-shaped sections on each leaf, and its yellow or white flower has five petals.

Primrose
Blooming in early spring, this delicate pale yellow flower is low-growing and spreads across the woodland floor like a carpet.

Ferns don't have flowers, but they are small plants that are easy to spot.

Violet
Wild violets have purple, heart-shaped petals and dark green leaves. They are tiny plants that don't mind shady ground.

Bramble
Bramble bushes grow into large hedgerows. They have pretty, pale flowers, and grow berries at the end of the summer. Blackberry brambles have prickly, thorny stems.

Poison ivy
Bees love the yellow flowers of this plant, but touching the leaves can give you a nasty, itchy rash.

Nightshade
These leafy plants can have beautiful flowers, but are often poisonous. One type, belladonna, is called deadly nightshade because it is so toxic.

TRY THIS...

FLOWER PRESSING
If you are careful, you can take a small number of flowers home and save them forever.

- Find the heaviest book on your bookshelf. Cut a piece of cardboard just smaller than the book.
- Lay a piece of newspaper onto the cardboard, then a piece of tissue paper.
- Arrange your flowers, spacing them out.
- Cover them with another piece of tissue paper and more newspaper.
- Place the whole thing between two pages of the book. Add another heavy book to weigh it all down.
- Check after a week to see if the flowers have dried.

Some flowers are protected by law, and you are not allowed to pick them. It is illegal to take flowers from federal land like national parks.

Yellow archangel
This plant is taller than many forest flowers and has lots of distinctive yellow and red blooms on each stalk.

WOODLAND WONDERS

Algae mostly live in water, but some are seen growing on tree trunks. They make their own food through photosynthesis.

Some things that live in the woodlands look like plants but don't have flowers, roots, or even proper leaves. These include algae and lichens as well as various types of fungi, which aren't plants at all.

Parasites

Fungi can't make their own food, so they live on other things and feed off them. Sometimes fungi break down rotting plants and creatures and return the nutrients to the soil. Other times, they kill the roots of a living tree so the tree cannot survive.

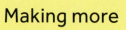

Puffball mushrooms release a cloud of spores into the air.

Making more

Most flowers reproduce by pollination. Pollen is carried between the flowers (on the wind, or by animals and insects), which then allows the flowers to grow seeds. Many types of fungi release microscopic **spores** instead of seeds. If they land in a moist place, they grow into new fungi.

Toadstools and mushrooms are types of fungi. Never pick and eat them in the wild as they may be poisonous.

Epiphytes

These are plants that grow on other living trees. Epiphytes absorb nutrients and moisture from the air and from the plant that supports them. Found in warm climates, they are also called air plants because they are not rooted in soil. Epiphytes are not parasites, but sometimes they grow very thick and damage their supporting plant.

Honey fungus spreads underground and attacks the roots of all kinds of plants.

TRY THIS...

MAKE A SPORE PRINT

The underneath of a mushroom is made of gills, like the spokes of a wheel. This is where the microscopic spores are stored. See it for yourself!

- Choose a large mushroom (buy them from a supermarket so you know they are safe to touch). Cut off the stem.
- Place the mushroom, face down, on a piece of white paper. (Use a glass microscope slide if you own a microscope.)
- Put a drop of water on top of the mushroom and then cover it with an upside-down glass or bowl. Leave it overnight.
- In the morning, you should have a print made by the falling spores.

WHAT'S IN A LOG?

Next time you leap over a log, stop instead and take a closer look. It will most likely be a home to all sorts of interesting things. Nature has a way of making use of everything, even if it is lying dead on the ground.

DID YOU KNOW?
These logs are called "nurse logs" because they support other living things.

Feeling rotten
A fallen log is no longer alive, but it can provide food and shelter for other living things. The log itself will begin to rot and will eventually become part of the soil. Many of the creatures that use the log will speed up the rotting process as they burrow into it and feed on it.

Rotting logs are a good water supply in dry weather. The moisture stays deep inside the wood.

Birds such as woodpeckers eat grubs and insects.

Some fungi grow with algae to form lichens. They aren't plants, even though they look plant-like.

Dry rot fungi and white-rot fungi digest the wood to make it decompose.

Bacteria help break down the wood into a powder, returning nutrients to the ground.

In late spring, look for white froth on plant stems. It is called cuckoo spit, and it contains a tiny white insect known as a froghopper.

A miniature world

A log is an example of a microhabitat: a tiny, specialized ecosystem in one particular type of place. An ecosystem is the collection of all the living things in an area, interacting with each other and their surroundings, including the sunshine, rain, temperature, and soil.

Moss is a simple plant that grows well in moist places.

Carpenter ants make their homes here, creating burrows called galleries.

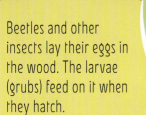

Beetles and other insects lay their eggs in the wood. The larvae (grubs) feed on it when they hatch.

TRY THIS...

MAKE A POOTER

Collect insects without having to pick them up with your hands. ALWAYS put them back where you found them afterward.

- You will need a see-through jar with a tight-fitting lid.
- Ask an adult to make two holes in the lid. They should be just big enough to fit a drinking straw.
- Fit a bendy straw in each hole and plug the gaps with clay.
- Cover the end of one straw with a square of gauze bandage or tights. Tape it in place.
- Replace the lid and try out your pooter. You should be able to point the uncovered straw at a grain of rice (or an insect) and suck at the covered straw hard enough for the rice to shoot up and into the jar.
- Collect one bug at a time and study it through the glass. Release it after a few minutes.

FINDING FOOD

The living things in a woodland interact with each other. A food chain shows what is consumed, or eaten, by what. For example, grass is eaten by a rabbit, which is eaten by a fox. A woodland has lots of food chains that join together to form a food web.

Woodland food web

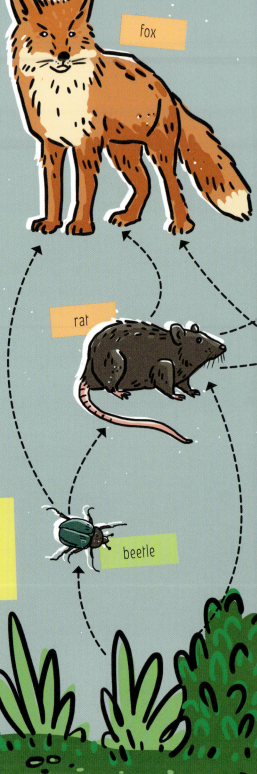

Producers and consumers

The first living thing in a food chain is a plant. The plants are known as **producers** because they make their own food from the sun. These are eaten by **herbivores**, such as grasshoppers, mice, rabbits, or deer. They are called primary **consumers**. Next come the secondary consumers that eat those creatures. The food chain can contain many consumers.

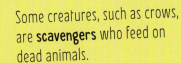

Some creatures, such as crows, are **scavengers** who feed on dead animals.

Top of the list

Animals that are at the end of the food chain are known as top predators or <u>apex predators.</u> They are creatures with no natural predators, such as eagles, owls, wolves, and bears.

owl

stoat

Fungi and bacteria are **decomposers** that break down material. They also feed on dead animals and plants.

rabbit

Losing a link

If one part of a food web is lost, it can affect all the other parts. If the grass dies during a drought, not only will the rabbits have no food, but the foxes will eventually have no rabbits to eat. Equally, if fox numbers decrease, they will not eat as many rabbits, and soon there will be so many rabbits that they will eat all of the grass.

PROTECTING OUR WOODLANDS

Many people are lucky enough to live close to a small wood. They are great places to study nature, play hiding games, and build forts. Some forests are much, much bigger and are in protected areas called national parks.

Huge numbers of trees are lost through deforestation.

National parks

The land and wildlife in a national park are protected by law. Most are open to the public, and you can camp or play and picnic in certain areas. Governments want people to respect and enjoy these beautiful wild places. Yellowstone National Park in the US has large areas of coniferous forest, while Sherwood Forest in the UK has deciduous trees that are hundreds of years old.

Yellowstone National Park

GOING, GOING, GONE!

There are around 3 trillion trees on Earth, covering almost a third of the land. That might sound like a lot, but now that billions of people live on the planet, we are cutting down millions of trees each year. If we aren't careful, we will lose too many of our precious forests and the planet will suffer.

Oxygen cycle

In the oxygen cycle, plants take in carbon dioxide and give out oxygen.

- photosynthesis
- carbon dioxide
- oxygen
- respiration

Why are forests important?

Forests are home to huge numbers of creatures, from tiny bugs to large mammals. The plants are used for medicines and cosmetics. Trees recycle the carbon dioxide that is produced when we breathe or burn fossil fuels and turn it back into the oxygen we need to survive. Their roots hold the soil together and stop the land from getting washed away during storms and floods.

WHAT CAN YOU DO?

Think about how you use paper. Recycle as much as you can, and go paperless where possible. Try to buy recycled items and products that have the FSC (Forest Stewardship Council) stamp on them. Plant a tree if you have the space, and most of all, enjoy trips to the woods where you can really appreciate the wonder and beauty of nature around you.

QUIZ

1. A forest takes many years to grow. What are the stages of its growth called?

a) expansion

b) succession

c) suspension

2. What do deciduous trees do?

a) change color in autumn

b) change shape in winter

c) change their position in summer

3. Hedgehogs sleep through winter to save energy. What is this long sleep called?

a) hibernation

b) preservation

c) vacation

4. An ash tree has compound leaves. This means the leaves:

a) are made up of several smaller leaflets

b) have several different shapes

c) fall off in winter

5. Conifer trees have what?

a) pins and needles

b) cones and needles

c) needles and thread

6. What is a microhabitat?

a) the part of a plant where seeds are found

b) where ants lay their eggs

c) a tiny, specialist ecosystem suited to a particular place

7. Plants are part of the food chain, and are called "producers." This means:

a) they make oxygen

b) they make water

c) they make their own food from sunlight

8. The woodland is full of flowers. Which one is is bell-shaped and fragrant, but also poisonous?

a) lily of the valley

b) lily of the mountain

c) water lily

Answers: 1 b, 2 a, 3 a, 4 a, 5 b, 6 c, 7 c, 8 a.

GLOSSARY

cambium one of the inner layers of a tree trunk that helps the tree grow

carnivore a creature that eats meat

compound leaf a leaf made up of several small leaflets

conifer a plant that protects its seeds inside cones

consumer in a food chain, a creature that eats plants or other creatures

deciduous a plant that loses its leaves in winter

decomposer an organism that breaks down organic material

evergreen a plant that keeps its leaves throughout the year

heartwood the inactive, central wood in a tree trunk

herbivore a creature that eats only plant-based food

hibernation a state of deep sleep to survive through the winter

migration seasonal movement from one location to another

photosynthesis the way green plants produce food

predator a creature that hunts and eats other creatures

producer the first part of a food chain, consisting of plants and algae

sapwood newly grown wood in a tree trunk

scavengers creatures that feed on things that are already dead

simple leaf a leaf with only one main part

spores the reproductive parts of some plants

succession the progressive stages of growth of a particular ecosystem

INDEX

acorn
6, 7

algae
15, 22, 24

bark
7, 14, 16, 17

chlorophyll
8, 11

cone
4, 6, 13, 14, 15, 17, 18

conifer
4, 6, 9, 12, 14, 18, 19

deciduous
4, 8, 11, 12-13, 16, 17, 20, 28

ecosystem
25

epiphytes
23

evergreen
4, 5, 8, 11, 14-15, 20

ferns
4, 11, 13, 20

food chain
26-27

forest fire
7, 15

fungi (fungus)
7, 13, 15, 22-23, 24, 27

hibernation
11, 16

lichen
13, 22, 24

moss
13, 15, 25

needles
4, 8, 9, 12, 14, 15

photosynthesis
8, 12, 22, 29

pollen
12, 22

FURTHER READING

These websites and books will give you lots more ideas about the great outdoors!

www.wildlifetrusts.org/about-us

www.fsc-uk.org/en-uk

www.woodlandtrust.org.uk/naturedetectives

www.rspb.org.uk/fun-and-learning/for-kids
  facts-about-nature

www.nationaltrust.org.uk/children-and-nature

www.discoverwildlife.com

www.fws.gov

Habitats (Outdoor Science)
Sonya Newland (Franklin Watts, 2019)

Trees (The Great Nature Hunt)
Clare Hibbert (Franklin Watts, 2019)

Woodland and Forest Animals (Saving Wildlife)
Sonya Newland (Franklin Watts, 2014)